Thriving through Covid-19

Copyright © 2021 Joelene Vallen
All rights reserved.

This book may not be reproduced in whole are in part, in any form or by any means, electronic, copy, recording, or by any information storage and retrieval system now known or hereafter without written permission from the publisher.

ISBN: 9798594287075
Imprint: Independently published

E book ASIN: B08SW13DCP

Contents

Introduction	5
Mindset & Leadership	7
Opportunities & Innovation	13
Optimize & Maximize	17
Additional Resources	21

Introduction

Are you struggling through the current Covid challenges? Through the recent coronavirus pandemic, I realized that many people were struggling to survive through the challenges presented as a result of the pandemic. Not only in their psychology but also within their businesses. As I successfully navigated a private healthcare practice through surviving the pandemic challenges and thriving through it, I felt I needed to share the strategies used with those who may be struggling in hopes that it will help them as well. In this book, we will cover mindset and leadership, innovation, optimizing and maximizing to not only survive but thrive through this pandemic. I believe everyone's dreams of success are attainable, even through the challenges we are currently up against.

NOW is YOUR time.

MINDSET & LEADERSHIP

All our beliefs and decisions are based on our mindset and whether we see our circumstances as victims or victors and whether we see current events as opportunities or devastation. How we choose to see things will direct our actions moving forward. You know the old saying "your thoughts become your words, your words become your actions, your actions become your habits, your habits become your character and your character becomes your destiny." What are your thoughts around the current events? How are those thoughts serving you? The first thing that comes to mind when I think about the subject is fear. We tend to go into fear when there is an area of uncertainty and in our current time there is a lot of uncertainty. How do we bring certainty to an area of so much uncertainty? People have asked me how I can possibly see any opportunity amid a national pandemic and widely different positions in a response and the future of our country. And my answer is, "where there is challenge there is always opportunity. Where there is fear, there is courage." By all means, I know this is easier said than done and we cannot just positively think ourselves into a different reality than the one we are living. I'm also not minimizing the current situation or the fear of uncertainty that surrounds us but what I am saying is we can operate from a different mindset. So, let us not focus on what we cannot change but rather put our time and energy into what we can change. The biggest advantage or hindrance in our lives or our business' is our psychology. Will things be different this next year? Likely yes but maybe some of those differences will be better than how we have been living. Our life today is different than that of ten years ago, some good differences and some not so good but at the end of the day we adjust and embrace the good to create the lives we want to live. I like to use technology as an example, some would say the advances in technology have brought great things and with it has come some not-so great things, generally speaking we embrace the good that it has brought. We make the choice to determine what it means to us and embrace its advantages. Ask yourself, what good has come to your life through this last year? Have you spent more time around the dinner table with your family? Have you grown closer to your friends? Have you served more in your community? Have you found more balance working remotely? Have you tapped into the opportunity of a virtual business? Have you mentally, physically or spiritually grown through this? Write down 3 to 5 good things that have happened recently. How have the changes this last year been working FOR you? What opportunities can you take advantage of that you had not thought of before? How can you pivot your business to meet the current needs out there? We can choose to thrive or suffer through this. Suffering is caused when we spend too much time thinking about what we have lost whereas thriving is when we choose to appreciate what we have. It is difficult to be angry and appreciative at the same time. What do you need to do to be comfortable in the areas of uncertainty you cannot control right now? Beliefs and values are the things that drive us, and we get to decide what we believe and value in life, in our jobs, with our families and in our relationships, so if something is not going well for us in those areas, I challenge you to ask yourself, what else could this mean? I clearly remember the day that Covid started to make an impact in my life. I was in a conference in Nashville and suddenly hand sanitizer was everywhere, people were not allowed to shake hands and there was a lot of conversation around the coronavirus and what it all meant. Upon returning home from the conference, I started paying attention to what other states were doing to manage the virus. As the leader of a healthcare company, I was not sure exactly how to navigate such a thing as nothing like this coronavirus response has ever been seen in my lifetime. As the leader it was my responsibility to not only determine the best action plan to navigate this for our staff, our doctors and our patients but also how we were going to keep our doors open. I knew immediately first and foremost I had to have the mindset that we were going to be ok through this and we were going to do everything we can to serve our patients. I also needed to be a voice of calm for our doctors, staff and patients as they were filled with uncertainty that came with the response to the coronavirus. In order to do this, I had to ensure my mindset was in the right place every day throughout confusion and not knowing what to do now and not knowing what was coming next, some days regulations and guidelines were changing by the hour. Since no one had really encountered a solution for such a challenge I was left to try and determine how we were going to make this happen. Every morning I started the day with reminding myself of the mission and ask myself, how can I continue to make decisions based on our mission, our values and that outcome. I knew a plan was our best defense in navigating this, so we came up with several. I immediately met with my CFO for a financial analysis six months out with several different scenarios and we came up with a plan of action that would be taken at each one of those scenarios. In addition, I knew cashflow may become a problem, so we accelerated our accounts receivables and decelerated accounts payables, we made preliminary arrangements with our vendors and our landlords, halted all nonessential spending and got creative in different scenarios of serving our patients all the while limiting the amount of people in one place at one time. My constant goal was to figure out a way to navigate this where we could still serve our patients with the highest quality of care without furloughing any staff or doctors as they are the heartbeat of our business. I am happy to say nine months into many Covid challenges, we were able to accomplish that goal. It took some creative strategies but more importantly it took the mindset of a leader to be able to remain calm and pivot to accomplish the goal and the desired outcome given the circumstances. Had I operated from a place of fear or from a place of scarcity I may not have been able to come up with the strategies and solutions that we were able to incorporate to not only survive but thrive through this very challenging time. We cannot solve a problem with the same level of thinking. Covid gave me an opportunity to grow in my level of thinking to solve the current problems. "Greatness comes from overcoming great challenges." A leader is someone who influences others. Leadership is the ability to step into another's world and impact them. A great leader must lead themselves first! In a situation like Covid whether you are the leader of your family, your team or your entire organization when no one knows what to do that is when you must be real and transparent with the sense of certainty to lead those depending on you. I was working as a CEO of a healthcare specialty clinic when Covid hit. It was one of the biggest challenges I have faced. Staff were coming to me from every angle wanting to know if they were going to lose their jobs, were we going to be able to continue providing care to our patients, what will we do about PPE and cleaning supplies, how do we decipher urgent and non-urgent situations? The mindset needed to lead through a tragedy is one of certainty and calm that I needed to provide to my team. Leadership is not just planning for today; leadership is planning for the possibilities of the future. Research shows 80% of success is psychology and 20% is strategy. That is why mindset is the area you want to check in with first. What would need to change in my psychology to be an effective leader? Is Covid really the obstacle? If we were to reframe the obstacle as an opportunity, how could we see it differently? Several leaders were able to not only survive the challenges of Covid but thrived because their psychology was that of not giving up. They got resourceful and learned how to pivot their business from the way they have always ran to something innovative and new providing what their customer needed most during this time. Research companies were able to spend more time on the ground without travel time by embracing virtual meetings allowing them to come up with new solutions in less time. Drive in movie theaters held virtual concerts and worked collaboratively with local theatres to show the movies that the traditional indoor theaters would have by sharing revenues with the local theaters. Grocery, retail and even convenience stores partnered with third party delivery services to meet their customers' needs and some have done so well in revenues in 2020 that they were able to afford to expand without acquiring debt. Restaurants got creative and some created drive throughs, delivery and take-out solutions, some even provided meal prep options and date night boxed food and wine for takeout, many have had more business than before. Healthcare companies provided curbside services and increased telemedicine visits and remote patient monitoring as well as home health services. One company's demand has grown so quickly that it is looking to hire 50 more people to meet the demand for their home health services. Gyms provided recorded streaming workouts and personal training that can be done at home without equipment. Coffee companies began offering coffee subscriptions by mailing their customers coffee beans to recreate their favorite drink at home. Several business' began making masks and distilleries began making hand sanitizer to supplement for the reduced alcohol purchases from restaurants and bars all the while helping fill the demand for these items. Telehealth companies have increased by over 50% and have had companies report 624% higher than expected in person volumes. Conference educators have provided their specialized knowledge by way of online courses and virtual conference events with the ability to serve more people at a reduced cost on both the presenter and the attendee. Therapists have utilized virtual therapy apps and online sessions to meet their client's needs. Digital behavioral health startups have spiked interest among investors attracting 588 million in funding the first half of 2020 whereas the same segment reached under that in the entire year of 2019. Local canneries were able to provide canned goods that grocery stores were selling out of.

As you can see several small business' and industries identified other areas of revenue or became resourceful in providing their services in another way that meets their customers' needs and are seeing more growth and revenues than ever before. But it had to start with a resourceful mindset. So, I ask you, Is this the end or the beginning?

OPPORTUNITIES & INNOVATION

Innovating for the greatest opportunities in today's time. Innovation is a word that is thrown around a lot today but what exactly does it mean? Innovation is simply the creation, development and implementation of a new product, process or service with the aim of improving efficiency, effectiveness or competitive advantage. In other words, how can you better serve your customer. I was on a call a few months back where a story was shared about a private practice that did not see the need to innovate through the years as their business was doing fine as is. Unfortunately, they recently closed their doors and went out of business over paper, yes, I said paper of all things. The paper vendors were shut down due to Covid shutdowns and paper was back ordered and they could not get their hands on any. Sounds similar to a recent toilet paper shortage. You may be asking yourself why would paper shut their doors? Well, they relied on paper for a new patient registration, patient intakes, copies of insurance cards, coding and billing sheets, prescriptions, handouts, referrals etc. Their inability to think ahead and be innovative even prior to Covid put them in a bind that all it took was the lack of production of paper to literally shut their doors. So, opportunities and innovation are not just a conversation amidst the Covid challenges that we face but we should be asking ourselves what areas could we innovate to better meet our customers' needs not just today but in the future? There will always be a company that comes around with an innovative idea. For example. Uber, brilliant business strategy the way they use other people's vehicles reducing their inventory, maintenance and liabilities while creating an app that is used for a convenient and less expensive mode of transportation than the taxi business that has been around since 1897 and is now on the brink of bankruptcy. I, myself travel a lot and rarely see anyone take a taxi anymore, Uber is less expensive and more convenient for me as a customer and customers want convenience in our world today. Uber, like Airbnb, Amazon and Facebook have become insanely successful by adopting innovative thinking and operating differently than that of what has been known. Or how about the famous video rental store Blockbuster, which although was a fun family experience on a Friday night to go pick out a movie together and have a pizza and movie night, did not make it once the convenience of next day mail and eventually at home streaming became accessible. Again, we are customers of convenience and it is much easier to have pizza delivered and stream the movie from our own TV. Blockbuster was unable to see the value in innovating for the future unfortunately. Where are they now? I believe that innovation is one of the most important factors to have on the forefront of any business that wants to survive long-term because the foundation of any business is to serve our customers and if we are not serving our customers by the convenience, need or want that they are looking for, we are not fully serving them. What areas could you improve to better serve your customer? What processes can be streamlined or automated to create efficiencies of time? What technologies can you adopt to provide a more convenient customer experience? What products and or services do your customers need right now that you can offer? Bring your team in on brainstorming solutions as they may have some great ideas to share. We must get honest when we are looking at this situation and stop hoping that the coronavirus will go away tomorrow and that we will miraculously all go back to business as usual. Innovation is at a pinnacle point, embrace its upside. Many business' have found success in employee's working from home by expanding their talent pool, lowering their overhead costs and increased employee productivity. In addition, it has been shown to increase employee satisfaction by living healthier lifestyles, improved work life balance, reduced costs and drivetime. A recent survey showed 55% of employers will continue remote work after the pandemic. Are there areas where you could implement remote work reducing costs and creating a win-win scenario? In order to fully see the opportunities and areas of innovation in our business we must know where we are first. Where is your business right now? What are the current strengths, weaknesses, opportunities and threats to your business? What is the value your business provides? How can you offer more value than others in your market? What do your customers need right now? Are you providing what the customers need in the current market? What roadblocks are keeping your company from moving forward? Once you have a clear idea of these areas you can begin to determine how and where innovation will serve you and your customers best. Think of your relationship with your customer. "Business is all about relationships." Do they need your product or service right now? How can you change the way you are providing the product or service to meet their needs? Is there a product or service you can offer that they need right now? Are you utilizing it to the capacity that it could be utilized, especially during such a virtual time? Are you marketing the services that your customers want and need? How efficient are your processes? Which areas could increase customers and sales? Innovation should be something that you incorporate into your culture within your team as something that you are constantly thinking about when reviewing your key performance indicators. Do not allow yourself or your team to get stuck in the mindset of the same ole same ole. You cannot create new solutions to problems with the same level of thinking. Tony Robbins mentions in his world class business mastery course, that in business sometimes you must rethink your approach, even those that have been successful, to create even bigger results. I have found this to be incredibly true as the world is constantly changing and with that so do the demands and needs of our customers, so why wouldn't we change our businesses to accommodate the needs of the customers that we serve?

OPTIMIZE & MAXIMIZE

Optimizing and maximizing for great success and profits. It is important to ensure sustainable processes and procedures are always functioning at peak efficiency for maximum optimization as this is a way to maximize your profits without adding revenues. If you are in business, you know how important operations are in the success of your business. What is even more important to your bottom line is that you are maximizing and optimizing the resources that you currently have, to take things to the next level by ensuring efficiencies that will create a more streamlined and profitable process. The easiest way to do this is to monitor your leading and lagging indicators or key performance indicators (KPI's), if you do not have key performance indicators, now is the time to create them, as it is difficult to monitor what we do not measure. In business decisions should always be made based on data. Make sure that you're creating specific KPI's to track your performance, revenues and profits and let them guide your business decisions and strategies. Think of your KPI or lagging indicator as your cholesterol or weight, your diet and exercise being your leading indicator or cause. Your cholesterol level or weight is the result of your diet and exercise. If your cholesterol level or weight is high, you must change your daily actions of diet and exercise to hit the ideal target number you are wishing to achieve. Your lagging indicator assesses the current or past level of business while your leading indicator predicts future outcomes. If your outcome is to lose 10 pounds or reduce your cholesterol level to the desired range, then you would set daily targets and determine your best actions to maximize your results and monitor them often. In business, last year's revenues and profits do not predict this year's revenues and profits as it is the daily actions that are the cause that affect those revenues and profits. Leading indicators would be your new products, customer satisfaction, new market growth, sales and employee satisfaction. Lagging indicators will tell you what has already happened like revenues, costs and profits. Focus on the outcomes you wish to achieve, set your leading and lagging indicators and continuously monitor them. If we are operating in a state of next level thinking, regardless of where we are, there is always a next level to achieve. In order to optimize and maximize what you already have, start by reviewing your current processes with your team and look for the areas that are out of the ideal range and work on process improvements. In the example above, the greatest impact may be a high cardio workout and a low calorie, low carb diet to achieve the desired result in the desired timeframe. Look for the areas that are under performing and create a plan to optimize and maximize those areas. Remember it is always important to keep asking your customers what they want as customer feedback is a vital KPI to measure. Identify your productivity constraints and implement new methods that are more efficient and cost effective but still produce a quality product or service. I recommend using the AIM system semi-annually. ANALYZE and optimize to make processes as effective as possible. IMPLEMENT new methods, processes and systems that reduce costs while improving performance. MONITOR your results to know where changes are working or where there is needed improvement to ensure peak efficiency. Is there an area you could automate for a streamlined workflow? Are there areas you can reduce waste in time or redundancy? What is a current process or service you could make changes to improve its usefulness? It does not necessarily have to be a new process or service but rather a more efficient or effective way to do it. This is an area where you may want to involve your teams' feedback or those doing the process. The goal is to create a consistent streamlined workflow and ensure a quality process to identify failures. What is the 20% of employees that produce 80% of the productivity doing differently? What is the 20% in your processes/procedures that accomplish 80% of your products or services? What is the 20% of time spent on creating 80% of revenues? Analyze and cut the fat in the areas that are not producing at the desired range. When was the last time you analyzed and adjusted operating costs? I like to look at optimizing in a simplistic way of achieving improved operating effectiveness and efficiencies and ensuring focus on the most effective 20% that gains you the 80% utilizing the 80/20 rule whereas 20% of your activities will account for 80% of your results. The 80/20 rule is a great way to identify where your 20% creating your 80% is and use them efficiently to create maximum value. 80% of your sales come from 20% of your workforce so make sure you are putting focus on the most effective 20% and replicate that. Again, using the analogy above, it's not the 100% of your day that is going to impact your cholesterol or weight, it is the 20% of your day spent intentionally on exercise and eating right that will, so make sure those areas are a priority. Where are some areas in utilization of space, products or sales you can make better use of? Where could you provide more levels of service or a product that compliments a current product? You see this when you go to a fast-food restaurant and they ask if you would like your meal super-sized, or when your server asks if you would like dessert, when an event offers a VIP experience, or you may have even seen over the holidays offerings such as if you spend $100.00 today you get a $20.00 gift card to spend later. These are all different levels of service and added value for your customer without adding much cost to you. Once you have done a thorough analysis of how you can better serve your customer by areas of improvement or offering new products or services you need to market those areas. Although marketing today is easier and cheaper than historically it is even harder to get noticed. Research shows it takes seven times before a customer remembers an advertisement. It takes repetition for a customer to remember what you have to offer so it is important to focus on repetition and frequency when it comes to marketing. Our digital world makes this easier by utilizing several different social media platforms. Think of some long-standing brands and jingles that have stuck through the years, we remember them because of repetition of seeing or hearing them like the lyrics to our favorite song or Nike just do it, American Express don't leave home without it or the jingle that would follow you through the day of Sleep Country USA why buy a mattress anywhere else. You just sang the jingle as you read it, didn't you? Apologies in advance if that jingle is stuck in your head throughout the rest of your day. We instinctually know these things because we have listened or seen their marketing strategies repeatedly and familiarity forms trust. Of course, we don't want to be the nagging spammer that constantly pops up with the same message over and over again on every social platform there is. Which is why I would always advise that your marketing have some type of value attached to it, like a solution you are providing to the current problem of your customers. Many years ago, I learned of the acronym WIFM and I have used it in many marketing strategies through the years. Your customers want to know "what's in it for me?" so put yourself in their shoes and create massive value for them. They want to buy something that will bring them value, that relates to them, touches them emotionally or makes sense logically. So, when you are marketing to your target audience, share a story that will relate to them and compel them to buy. Hopefully you have seen throughout this book, that If we see this time as an opportunity and innovate to meet our customers' needs, we may just find an opportunity to take our business to a whole new level.

NOW IS YOUR TIME.

If you are looking for a partner in helping you achieve your attainable goals, you can contact Attainable Success LLC for a free consultation by emailing us at
attainablesuccessllc@gmail.com

Attainable Success provides Business Consulting services as well as Personal Development coaching to help you grow to your next level.

Attainable Success LLC provides consulting and coaching in the areas of Strategic growth, Human Resources, Operations and Leadership development.

Also be sure to check out The Attainable Success Podcast for inspiring stories of success in areas of parenting, relationships, business, health and personal development.

www.attainablesuccessllc.com @ATTAINABLE_SUCCESS

Would you like to have Joelene Vallen speak at your event or with your team?

Author Joelene Vallen believes in a world where everyone's dreams of success are attainable. As a business strategist who has studied in business and leadership for over 20 years, Joelene brings a unique skill of innovative and resourceful strategies to help leaders and companies grow to the next level. She has a proven executive management track record with a wealth of knowledge and success in streamlining operations for maximum efficiencies and optimization, strategic solutions for growth, risk mitigation, change management and human resources.

To inquire about having Joelene speak at your event or your business please visit **www.joelenevallen.com** or email us at **attainablesuccessllc@gmail.com**

www.ingramcontent.com/pod-product-compliance
Lightning Source LLC
Chambersburg PA
CBHW050329220526
45465CB00005B/2206